Tavernspite CP
Tavernspite, Whitlar
Tel: 01834 83:

CW01336530

DIRK OF SWAMPY HOLLOW

Emma Barnes

Illustrated by Lee Cosgrove

OXFORD
UNIVERSITY PRESS

Welcome to the world of Dirk! Dirk's Stone Age is not like one you will find in any other book: no, it's full of all kinds of beasts whose fossilized remains have yet to be discovered, and about which any palaeontologist would declare, 'Snaggle-Toothed Swamp Cat? You've got to be kidding!' But let's not worry about that, or whether swamps would exist next door to icy mountains, or whether wolves could communicate with humans, or whether prehistoric people ever wore sun cream. After all, Dirk's not bothered. He's got other things on his mind ...

Chapter 1
No Good Dirk

Dirk lived in a stone house. He ate his meals off stone plates. He slept on a stone bed. And when he had a bath he took it ... in a muddy hole in the ground. (Who's going to build a stone bathtub that's only used once a year?)

Dirk lived in Swampy Hollow, a highly desirable Stone Age neighbourhood in the middle of a swamp. Half the homes were built from sticks and leaves. Their owners considered them the best because:

1. They were air-conditioned (the wind blew through the gaps).
2. They had running hot and cold water (the swamp water ran in under the walls, and if you could somehow manage to get a fire going, the water soon warmed up). Also, you never ran out of firewood: if supplies were low, you could always burn down the porch.

The other half of the village lived in caves. They considered their homes to be the best because:

1. Mammoths could not push them over.
2. They did not have hot and cold water running through the middle of the floor.
3. You could build a fancy porch out of boulders which would make all your neighbours really jealous – unless a mammoth pushed it over.

Admittedly, sometimes there were bats living in the caves, but who doesn't want a vampire bat as a pet?

Like every regular Stone Age kid, Dirk spent endless hours gathering berries, collecting firewood, scavenging, knapping flints (which means making them pointy), napping under a bush (because he was tired from the flint-knapping), fishing, fetching water, yawning in front of the fire while his dad told one of his interminable stories, looking out for mammoths, being told by his parents and teachers to stop gawping, and being asked why he hadn't done his homework on time.

The thing he didn't get to do was hunting.

'You have to prove yourself first,' his dad would say.

'How can I prove myself if I'm not allowed to hunt?' Dirk would ask. But his dad would just pretend to have a bit of mammoth gristle stuck in his teeth.

One afternoon, Dirk was plodding home from school. He was alone. The kids of Swampy Hollow were not supposed to walk anywhere unaccompanied on account of the bristly bears, toe-biting badgers, stampeding mammoths, fanged water voles, poisonous snakes and all the other perilous wildlife in the area. But today Dirk didn't care.

'Couldn't stand walking with Muzzy today,' he muttered. 'She's such a show-off. Always going on about how wonderful she is. "Oh, look at this flint I knapped!"' He pretended to be Muzzy. '"Look how pointy it is! Look, what a neatly knapped edge! I expect I'm the best flint-knapper in the whole of Swampy Hollow!"'

Dirk waded through a stream, ignoring the bouncing bullfrogs.

'As for Brabbin,' he went on, 'he's not exactly a show-off. He's my best friend, but he *is* still Chief Windabag's son. People take him seriously. He doesn't know how it feels to be No Good Dirk, like me.'

'BOO!'

Dirk nearly jumped out of his skin. (Well, he didn't

really – it's actually impossible unless you're a snake or a lizard, and even then it has to be the right time of year.) Instead, he tripped over a tree root and landed in squelchy mud.

'Ahhhh!' he yelled. 'Mammoths! Please don't squash me! Trample me gently!'

He heard a snort of derisive laughter. 'Ooh, Dirk, you are funny!' trilled a voice. 'Mammoths don't say boo! They don't say anything. They just make a snorty noise and wave their trunks.'

It was Muzzy. She cavorted around the trees, waving her left arm, pretending to be a mammoth.

'All right, all right,' said Dirk, getting up. 'Actually, I know just as much about mammoths as you do, Muzzy. More, in fact – my cousin Faffy's entire village got squashed in a mammoth stampede.'

They headed off towards home. Muzzy was skipping cheerfully but Dirk just trudged. Something was weighing on his mind. (It was also weighing on his shoulders.)

'I wish school wasn't finished,' said Muzzy, still skipping. 'But I've got lots of plans for the summer. I'm going to finish my berry collection. I've got thirty-five different types so far, did you know that? There's crimson ones, and purple ones, and maroon ones with pink flecks, and pink ones with maroon flecks, and enormous big hairy ones ... '

'Huh,' said Dirk in a loud voice.

'And of course, my parents are going to be absolutely delighted with my report!' Muzzy continued.

Dirk felt like a mammoth had just kicked him in the stomach. This was what had been weighing on his mind, and his shoulders. His school report. As it was in the form of a heavy stone tablet, he was getting sick of lugging it around – but he didn't want to hand it over to his parents either!

'What do you want to do this summer, Dirk?' asked Muzzy.

'I want to go hunting,' said Dirk rashly.

Muzzy nearly fell over laughing. 'Nobody will let you do that. Do you know what my dad said? He said, "If Dirk ever went mammoth hunting then the mammoths would probably end up hunting him!"'

'Well, you just wait and see!' Dirk yelled. 'I'm going to be the best mammoth hunter in the whole of Swampy Hollow!' And he ran off in the direction of his own cave.

Chapter 2
School report

Dirk had intended to wait until his mum and dad were in a good mood before presenting them with his school report: after supper, maybe, when they were relaxed and replete with mammoth kebabs. He'd even find them some honeycomb as a treat. Then he'd introduce the subject slowly ...

It would have been a great plan, except that he was so busy planning it that he wasn't looking where he was going, and so the first thing he did on entering the cave was to bump into his dad and drop the report on his foot.

'OW!' yelled his dad, red-faced with pain and fury. 'Watch what you're doing, you great lump of bear bristle, you! You – you mammoth toenail! You clod-hopping, beetle-brained, fish-faced wombat!'

He really was *hopping* mad. In fact, he could have beaten a rabbit in a hopping competition.

'Sorry, Dad,' said Dirk.

'*Sorry*?' roared his dad. 'You've broken every bone in my foot.'

'Oh, nonsense,' interrupted Dirk's mum. 'You're a big baby sometimes, Offa! I think you make more fuss than Dumpa – and she's not even two yet!'

While his parents were distracted by squabbling, Dirk took the opportunity to pick up his report. He was hoping that it had shattered into a thousand pieces. But it hadn't. It wasn't even chipped.

Typical, thought Dirk.

'What is that thing, anyway?' demanded his mum. 'You haven't been stealing bits of next door's porch again, have you? I know you kids think it's funny, but it was no laughing matter that time it collapsed on top of Grandad Beeswax ... he's still looking lopsided, if you ask me.'

'It's my school report,' Dirk said.

'Then hand it over!'

It took a while for Dirk's parents to read the report, on account of how it was all written in squiggles and strange pictures.

'What does *this* mean?' they wondered, holding it upside down. 'What's *that* meant to be?'

'Looks like a *worm*.'

'Well, why'd they put a worm on his report?'

'Maybe his teacher thinks he *is* a worm.'

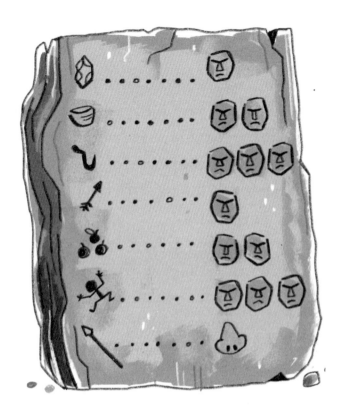

'Well, that's not very nice, is it, even if he *does* think so?'

Eventually they began to remember some of the stuff they had learned back in their own school days, and the report started to make sense. They took it in turns to read it out.

'Flint-knapping,' read Dirk's mum. 'Bad.'

'Pot-throwing: very bad.'

'Fishing: very, very bad.'

'Oh, so that's what that worm thing is – it's a fish hook,' said Dirk's dad.

'Arrow-making: bad,' continued Dirk's mum.

'Berry-gathering: very bad.'

'War-dancing: very, very bad. And what's that mean? Looks like a nose?'

'Maybe it means so bad it stinks?' said Dirk's dad.

'Ah, that makes sense. Spear-throwing: so bad it stinks.'

When they had finished, they stared at Dirk.

'Aren't you good at *anything*?' asked his mum. 'Even your big brother Grunk was good at something.'

'No, he wasn't,' said Dirk's dad.

'Yes, he was. He was good at rock-breaking. On account of the fact he's so big.'

'Oh, that's right. He just had to jump on them.'

Dirk said, 'I'm not good at anything *in* school. But there are loads of things I'm good at *out* of school. Anyway, Old Dustabin doesn't like me – everyone knows that. Besides, I expect most people's reports were terrible.'

'What about Muzzy?' asked his mum immediately. Dirk said nothing. Muzzy always got 'Excellent' for *everything*.

'Now, let me tell you, Dirk—' his mum began, but luckily at that moment his little sister Dumpa started squawking because she had lost the tug of war she was having with Cross Eye the dog over an old mammoth bone. Mum confiscated the bone, and then thankfully everyone was distracted for a while organizing dinner. Dirk's dad stirred the pot, while Mum fetched the plates. Grunk came in and was sent to collect more firewood, and Dirk was instructed to keep an eye on Dumpa, who was crawling round and round the cave.

I wish I was as big as Grunk, thought Dirk, *even if I did keep bumping my head on the cave roof.*

Grunk was breaking the firewood by squeezing it in his fists. If there was an especially big branch, he sat on it.

Of course, Faffy's not good at anything, thought Dirk, as his cousin came in. *But nobody minds. You can get away with anything if you're lucky enough to have your entire village flattened in a mammoth stampede*!

The next moment, Grunk tipped a pile of wood on to the fire, smothering it. Before Dirk's dad had time to finish yelling, 'You oafish great lump of oafishness, you,' Faffy had knelt down, rubbed a couple of sticks together and reignited the flames.

That's when Dirk remembered that Faffy was absolutely the best fire-lighter in the whole of Swampy Hollow.

He sighed. *At least Dumpa's not good at anything*, he thought. *Not yet, anyway.*

'Dirk, where's your sister?' called his mum. 'Go look for her! You know perfectly well she's the fastest crawler in Swampy Hollow!'

Dirk jumped up and ran out of the cave where he caught up with Dumpa just before she reached the forest.

Even Dumpa's good at something, he thought, as he carried the wriggling baby back to the cave. *It's just me that isn't*!

***

Over dinner, Dirk's parents gave him the usual lecture on how he had to change his attitude, pull himself up by his bearskin belt, give himself a good kick and Do Much, Much Better In Future.

'I want to go hunting,' said Dirk. 'I'm sure I'd be

good at that. Now that school's finished, please can I go on a hunting trip?'

There was a long silence. Neither of his parents looked enthusiastic.

'Maybe you *should* take him,' said his mum to his dad at last.

'Are you joking? Why don't you take him hunting, if you're so keen on the idea?'

'Of course, I was a wonderful hunter, before we had children,' said his mum nostalgically. 'But now everything's different.'

'Why is it different?'

'Well, *you* try looking after a cave and four children every day. I often wish I *did* have the chance to go hunting and get some fresh air and exercise.'

'Then off you go and have a lovely day out,' said Dad, 'and *I'll* look after the cave.'

'Oh, I see what you're up to – don't think I don't!'

They fell to squabbling, but one thing was clear: neither of them was prepared to take Dirk anywhere near a mammoth hunt.

That night Dirk went to bed miserably aware that his dreams of being a great hunter were just that – dreams. He was fated to be No Good Dirk forever.

But the next morning, everything changed. Brabbin came running over, full of excitement, because his dad, Chief Windabag, had had a new idea. He told Dirk it was called Work Experience. It meant that, now school was over, all the older kids should go out with the grown-ups and help with the jobs they did. Even better, the kids could choose what they wanted to do.

'Hear that, Dad?' yelled Dirk. 'I'm going mammoth hunting after all!'

Chapter 3
The mammoth hunt

Most of the grown-up villagers thought Work Experience was a dreadful idea. They didn't want their kids getting underfoot, they said: the whole point of work was getting away from them! They thought it was such an outrageous notion that they made their feelings clear to Chief Windabag.

There was a big village meeting, with a lot of speeches, and even some shouting, but in the end Chief Windabag got his way.

'The trouble with that man is he loves the sound of his own voice,' grumbled Dirk's dad, later. 'You can't win an argument with him because he just keeps waffling.'

'Of course he does,' said Dirk's mum. 'That's why he's the chief. He's full of hot air.'

'But doesn't being chief mean he's wise?' asked Dirk.

Dirk's mum almost fell over laughing. 'Wise? If we wanted someone wise, we'd choose Old Wrinkly One. Everyone knows she's the wisest person in Swampy Hollow, as well as the oldest. The trouble is she's too wise to take the job!'

At breakfast next morning, Dirk's dad did his best to put Dirk off the whole mammoth-hunting idea.

'You know, son, mammoth hunting isn't all it's cracked up to be. Especially in bad weather: you can get fungus-foot from squelching through swamps, and terrible spear-elbow too. Why don't you try something else, like, say – cooking?'

'No,' said Dirk firmly. 'I'm going hunting.'

'But think how dangerous it is! I mean, have you ever wondered what happened to Bruggalump's ear?'

'No,' Dirk admitted. 'What happened?'

'A lion happened. And why does your Aunty Gragga have nine toes, eh?'

'Why?'

'Because a crocodile took a nibble. And as for Lopsided Lugga's left—'

'Not over breakfast!' interrupted Dirk's mum.

'What about Kylar Spear Arm?' asked Dirk, naming the most famous hunter in their village.

'What about him?'

'Well, what happened to his other arm?'

'Nothing,' said his dad. 'He was born that way. You don't think a hunter like Kylar would ever get caught out, do you? But as for *you*, Dirk – you'll end up as a mammoth's lunch if you're not careful!'

But Dirk had made up his mind. A few days later, the villagers received word of a herd of mammoths in the area and a hunting party gathered. Kylar Spear Arm was there, naturally, because he was the best hunter in the village. Chief Windabag and Dirk's dad were also there, as well as Dirk, Brabbin and Muzzy, all clutching their new spears.

'Our aim,' Kylar Spear Arm told them, 'is to hunt down a mammoth. And the important thing is – what?'

'Not to get trampled,' said Muzzy quickly.

'Wrong!' (Muzzy, who was never wrong, gasped.) 'The important thing is to hunt it down before that sneaky lot from Boggy Dell get there. They'll be trying to beat us to it, you mark my words.'

Boggy Dell was the next-door village, and there was an ancient rivalry between the neighbours. The idea that the 'Boggers' (as the Swampy Hollow villagers called the Boggy Dell dwellers) might get a mammoth first enraged the hunters. 'We'll beat those scaredy-cats – that bunch of marsh frogs – those knock-kneed swamp weasels, you see if we don't!' they cried.

'Now remember,' Kylar went on, 'we only need one mammoth. We'll pick out the weakest one and separate it from the herd.'

'But won't that mammoth still be lots stronger than us?' chirped up Brabbin.

'Of course it will. But we're not going to *fight* the mammoth. We herd it towards the cliffs by making noises all round it, like this!'

Kylar Spear Arm made a low growling noise, like a lion or a tiger. 'GRRRRRR!'

Then he banged two rocks together. CRASH! CRASH!

Finally, he made a loud stamping noise with his feet. BOOM! BOOM!

'The mammoth panics! It starts to run! We close in on it. We herd it towards the cliff and over the edge it goes!'

'And once the clean-up crew has done their job at the bottom of the cliff, it's mammoth kebabs all round,' put in Dirk's dad happily.

Everyone cheered, except Dirk. He couldn't help thinking it was a bit sneaky to trick it into falling off a cliff. 'Isn't that a bit – well – unfair?' he asked.

Everybody looked at him.

'What do *you* suggest?' asked Kylar.

'Well – er – I thought we could fight it with our spears.'

Everybody collapsed with laughter. '*You* fight it with your spear,' gasped Chief Windabag. 'I'd give up my best flint to see that! I'd give my whole flint collection for a front-row seat!'

Dirk went red. Soon after, they set off. At first Dirk was full of excitement. But as they got further and further from Swampy Hollow, he began to get fed up. His feet hurt. His spear was heavy. And he was hungry.

What I wouldn't give for a kebab, he thought. *Or even a frog on a stick*!

22

He found himself at the back of the party. Chief Windabag was there, too. He told Dirk that it was essential for an especially fierce hunter to bring up the rear in case a wild animal attacked from behind.

Suddenly, Kylar Spear Arm held up his hand. 'Hush!'

Everyone hushed.

Kylar pointed. Through the trees ahead, they saw open grassland, and across the grassland, a herd of mammoths grazing.

Dirk held his breath. He'd never seen a mammoth so close before – never mind twenty all at once. They were enormous! Their legs were as thick and strong as ancient tree trunks. Their tusks were as white and curved and sharp as ... well, as something you wouldn't want heading towards your tummy. Above all, they were hairy. Why, they were even hairier than Grunk!

Kylar Spear Arm turned and made a gesture with his hand. It meant – Start Spreading Out.

The hunters started spreading out.

Kylar made another gesture. It meant – Start Tiptoeing Forward.

The hunters started tiptoeing forward.

Kylar held up his hand again. This time it meant –
Wait, While I Choose the Weakest Mammoth. But
before he could even get started ...

KERPLUNK!

Everyone stared at Dirk.

'Er, sorry,' Dirk whispered. 'I dropped my spear.'

'You clumsy hippo,' hissed his dad.

Before anyone else could tell him off, Brabbin
pointed at the mammoths. 'Watch out!'

The mammoths, alerted by the noise of Dirk's spear clattering to the ground, had stopped grazing and were stampeding towards them.

'RUN FOR YOUR LIVES!' yelled Kylar.

So they did.

Dirk kept dropping his spear, so in the end he abandoned it. *Perhaps it will trip up a mammoth*, he thought hopefully. *That will give me a few extra seconds before being squashed.* He ran on. Everyone else seemed a long way ahead already, sprinting towards a copse.

The breath was tearing in Dirk's chest. His heart was pounding. His legs were burning. *I can't run a step further*, he thought, but then he happened to glance over his shoulder. There was a mammoth right behind him. Its little red eyes glared balefully at Dirk and there was steam coming from its trunk. *Maybe I can run after all*, thought Dirk.

TRUMPET, TRUMPET, TRUMPET! went the mammoth.

TARUMP, TARUMP, TARUMP! went the sound of its feet.

The mammoths were gaining. The mammoths were almost on him ...

Suddenly, Dirk's legs gave way beneath him. *This is it*, thought Dirk. *I'm for it. Squashed. Trampled. Pulverized. This really wasn't what I had in mind for my first hunt*!

He shut his eyes tightly. After a few moments, he noticed to his surprise that he was still unsquashed. Then he realized that it wasn't his legs that had given way but the ground beneath him, and he had fallen into a small ditch. When Dirk stuck his head out of the ditch a few moments later, it was to the sight of twenty enormous, hairy mammoth bottoms disappearing into the distance.

He'd never seen anything so wonderful in his whole life.

I hope the rest of the hunters escape too, he thought. He was optimistic that they would. They were all much faster runners than him and good at hiding in the undergrowth. He gave a happy sigh.

His happiness was short-lived.

Something was moving close by, in the ditch. It was moving slowly, surreptitiously, as if it did not want to be heard ... and it seemed to be creeping up on Dirk!

Chapter 4

Lost

Dirk trembled like a leaf on a frozen branch. He wondered what creature was with him in the ditch.

A bristly bear?

A ravening wild goat?

Or ... worst of all ... could it be the dreaded Snaggle-Toothed Swamp Cat? He had never seen one, but everyone knew they existed and that they were the deadliest, most dangerous, most terrifying creatures that dwelt anywhere in the vicinity of Swampy Hollow. Dirk was so terrified that his knees were knocking and his hands were shaking. For a moment, too, he suspected something even worse might have happened, but then he realized it was just that the ditch was a bit soggy.

Come on, Dirk, he told himself. *There's no point sitting here and waiting to be eaten. You've got to be brave. You've got to attack first*!

He hoisted up a hefty chunk of wood from the bottom of the ditch. Then he took a deep breath – and charged!

'HEYAAAAAH!' yelled Dirk, bashing away with his improvised club.

The creature squeaked and backed away into the shadows. Dirk thumped it some more.

'Take that, you loathsome worm! And that!'

'Ouch!' yelled the creature. 'Watch out! That's my nose!'

It wasn't a wild and ravening beast after all. It was Chief Windabag.

They stared at each other for a moment.

'What are you doing?' Dirk asked.

'What do you mean? Don't you know there are mammoths out there?' Chief Windabag's voice was a bit muffled because he was holding his nose. 'It was very clever of me finding this ditch.'

'You mean you're *hiding*?' asked Dirk, astonished. 'But you're an experienced hunter! You're the chief of our whole village! You should be out there defending everyone else!'

'Well, you're hiding too.'

'I fell in here by mistake!'

'Oh. I see.' Chief Windabag looked a bit embarrassed. 'Well, retreat is the best form of attack, you know. And – er – better safe than sorry.'

'But you were even scared of *me*,' Dirk pointed out.

'I wasn't,' protested Chief Windabag. 'At least, I didn't know it was *you*. It sounded like someone *much* bigger. I thought it might be one of those Boggers, or a sabre-toothed hamster or something. Anyway, I wasn't hiding, I was just waiting to – er – jump out at you. Then when I saw it was only you – well, it didn't seem worth the trouble.' Chief Windabag clutched his bleeding nose. 'I don't suppose you've got any fresh moss, have you?' he asked pathetically.

For the next couple of hours, Dirk and Chief Windabag crouched in the ditch. Chief Windabag dabbed his bleeding nose with moss and regaled Dirk with tales of his valour on other mammoth hunts (although Dirk wasn't sure he believed them). Every now and then Dirk suggested they should go and look for the rest of their hunting party, but Chief Windabag always said no, *much* better to wait, and, who knows, if they only waited long enough maybe the other hunters would find *them*.

Eventually, they did crawl out of the ditch. By this time, it was getting dark. Neither of them was sure which direction they should be going, but they were cold and tired and stiff, their stomachs were grumbling, and they were both fantasizing about a hot meal and a warm fire.

'I think it might be that way,' said Dirk, pointing.

'Nonsense!' declared Chief Windabag. 'That's quite wrong. You just follow *me*. When you've been on as many hunting trips as I have, you can tell which way is home just by the smell of the wind, or by seeing which sides of the trees have moss growing on them.'

'But there's no wind blowing and there aren't any trees here,' Dirk pointed out.

'That's quite enough cheek from you!' Chief Windabag strode off, and Dirk had little choice but to follow.

After a while, though, Chief Windabag had to concede that they didn't seem to be getting any closer to home. So they changed direction, but that was no good either. Soon they were thoroughly lost.

They were trailing despondently through a small wood, wondering where on earth they were, when they heard something. 'Grrrrr!'

'Did you hear that?' whispered Chief Windabag shakily.

'It sounded like a growl ... '

'That's what I thought.'

Dirk looked at Chief Windabag to see what they should do next, but all Chief Windabag was doing was quivering like a giant jellyfish.

Then they heard a new noise, a bit like banging rocks.

CRASH! CRASH!

'That must be a very big animal to make such a loud noise,' said Dirk.

Chief Windabag just shook even harder.

And finally: STAMP! STAMP!

'Whatever kind of animal that is, there must be a lot of them,' said Dirk. 'That sounds like *hundreds* of feet.'

'Run for it!' Chief Windabag didn't wait for Dirk, but hurtled off into the distance.

Dirk ran too. But as he ran, something was nagging at the back of his mind.

Growling. Banging rocks together. Stamping feet.

What did that remind him of?

Of course!

He slid to a halt. 'Wait a minute!' he yelled. 'We're being *herded*! There's a bunch of mammoth hunters out there and they're trying to herd us over the cliffs!'

'Nonsense!' yelled Chief Windabag over his shoulder. 'All our hunters will have gone home long ago. We *never* stay out overnight. We always like to get back in time for supper at Swampy Hollow ... AHHHHHHHHH!'

With that, Chief Windabag went over the cliff.

Dirk approached the edge cautiously. He couldn't hear anything and he feared the worst for Chief Windabag. A few minutes later, though, there came the sound of shouting and yelling – Chief Windabag had obviously got his breath back. He hadn't actually fallen that far, and was now lying in a pile of spiky bushes.

'What the – *harrumph* – *grunt* – of all the – can't somebody – *grumphf* – I've got thorns in embarrassing places! And I'm stuck!'

Dirk collapsed with laughter. 'Just look at Chief Windy!' he gasped to the hunters who had come up behind him. 'He's fallen into thorn bushes and got prickles in his – *oh*.' Dirk stopped short, because he had just realized he didn't recognize the hunters who were gathered around him, carrying burning torches and spears. He couldn't see his dad or Kylar Spear Arm, or Muzzy and Brabbin, anywhere.

Slowly he realized the horrible truth. These weren't the hunters from Swampy Hollow – these were the hunters from Boggy Dell!

***

The Boggy Dell hunters recognized Chief Windabag straight away, but they pretended they didn't. They pretended that they thought Dirk and Chief Windabag were dangerous enemies who had to be taken prisoner. In the end, Chief Windabag had to promise to give the Boggers four mammoth rugs, three stone axes and two cooking pots as a reward for letting them go.

The villagers of Swampy Hollow were pleased to see that Dirk and Chief Windabag were safe. They were less pleased that it was their rivals from Boggy Dell who had brought them home again. They were absolutely furious about the four mammoth rugs, three stone axes and two cooking pots they had to give in exchange for getting back their careless chief and one troublesome boy!

The Boggers made the most of their triumph. They made jokes about how Chief Windabag was the slowest, smelliest mammoth they had ever hunted, and Dirk the puniest mammoth calf.

'Old Windabag looked more like a porcupine by the time we pulled him out of those thorn bushes,' joked one of the hunters.

Chief Windabag tried to put a brave face on things. He even made a speech to the Boggers. 'Thank you, kind neighbours,' he said. 'You have won our everlasting gratitude. The hand of friendship has been extended between our two villages, and a warm welcome awaits all of you whenever you come to Swampy Hollow!'

'Not if I see you first, it doesn't,' muttered Kylar Spear Arm, while the rest of the villagers growled.

The Boggers left, congratulating themselves for having got one over on their rivals, and gloating over all the good things they were taking back with them. Dirk went home to a hot supper and bed.

He was a bit disappointed at the way his first hunting trip had turned out. Still, at least the other villagers weren't laughing at him and saying how useless he was. They were far too busy laughing at Chief Windabag!

Chapter 5
Dirk's good idea

That was the end of Work Experience. It wasn't just the mammoth-hunting trip that had gone wrong. All the grown-ups in the village were full of complaints about holes in fishing nets, and capsized boats, and broken flints, and burnt dinners. As for the kids, they said that even school had been more fun than being bossed around all day by their parents.

So for a while Dirk and his friends were left alone to enjoy their summer holidays, just so long as they did their usual chores too. Only nothing ever went quite to plan.

It was fishing season, and Dirk was very proud when he managed to catch a carp with his bare hands – only to have it wriggle through his fingers and bounce off his head into the river again!

When they went gathering honeycomb, it was Dirk who disturbed a nest of giant hornets, which pursued them all the way home.

When they went gathering eggs, it was Dirk who climbed too high up a tree and got stuck, and Muzzy who climbed up to rescue him. Later that same day Dirk tripped over a tree root – and sat on the eggs!

'You're a bit of a gurk, Dirk!' Muzzy told him.

'What's a gurk?' asked Dirk, attempting to wipe off the egg yolks.

'A gurk is a word I just invented for somebody like you who always messes up!'

'Huh,' said Dirk. 'Well, I'd rather be a gurk than a gizzy-guzzy.'

Muzzy didn't say anything. Dirk could see she was bursting to know what a gizzy-guzzy was, but didn't want to admit she didn't know. He smiled to himself.

At last Muzzy could stand it no more. 'What's a gizzy-guzzy?'

'It's a word I just made up for describing an annoying know-it-all like you!'

Still, Dirk couldn't help brooding over what Muzzy had said. He was still pondering it that evening as he had dinner with his family. Everyone was there except Faffy. Dirk's mum doled out the food (tonight it was stewed fish from the river, with a side helping of wild mushrooms) and bellowed, 'Faffy! FAFFY! HOW MANY TIMES DO I HAVE TO CALL YOU?'

She turned to face the rest of the family, whose ears were now all ringing.

'That girl! Always with her head in the clouds! I know her entire village was trampled in a mammoth stampede, but still – is that any excuse for always mooning around?'

'Well ... ' said Dirk's dad, but at that moment Faffy came wandering in. Everyone watched as she sat down and ate her food listlessly. She didn't speak to anybody, just sighed a lot and tossed her hair. After a while she pushed away her plate and wandered off, holding a big seashell to her ear.

'Now, isn't that typical?' said Dirk's mother. 'Of course, they are difficult, the teenage years.' She pointed at Grunk. 'I mean, look at him! Hairy, clumsy, smells like a decaying antelope. Sleeps the whole morning, unless I kick him out of bed. Can't speak – only grunts.'

'Nofffair,' grunted Grunk.

'See what I mean?' said Dirk's mum. 'But I think Faffy is worse. Only interested in scratching messages to her friends on that stupid tablet of hers. And she always has that seashell glued to one ear. She'd rather listen to the sounds it makes than talk to us! And now she seems to have gone off my cooking!'

'Maybe she needs something to cheer her up and take her mind off things?' suggested Dirk's dad. 'Like ... a mammoth hunt?' They all looked at him incredulously. 'OK, so not a good idea,' he said hastily.

There was a long pause. Suddenly, Dirk jumped up (knocking his food over Cross Eye as he did so).

'I know! Why don't we go to the seaside? That would take her mind off things!'

There was a pause. Then his mum said, 'Do you

know what, Dirk, that's actually a really good idea. Faffy loves swimming and gathering shells.'

Dirk glowed with pride. Surely a gurk would never have had such a brilliant idea? 'It was that seashell she listens to that made me think of it,' he explained modestly.

'What do the rest of you say?' Dirk's mum asked.

'Yunk,' said Grunk through a mouthful of Faffy's leftover fish, so everybody took that as a 'yes'.

'Bubba bubba bub!' said Dumpa, and they took that as a 'yes' too.

Cross Eye the dog waved his tail.

The only one who wasn't in favour was Dirk's dad. 'First we have to get to the sea – and it's about five days' walk from here. We could easily get attacked and eaten on the way. Then we don't know if we'll find enough food. Finally, the sea is full of dangers. We could be attacked by sharks or poisoned by jellyfish or even carried out to sea by a terrible, tentacled sea monster.'

'How you do fuss about little things!' said Dirk's mum airily. So that settled it. The next day, packing commenced.

HOLIDAY LIST

FURRY BATHING COSTUMES

SUN CREAM (MADE FROM BEST QUALITY
  MAMMOTH FAT)

A TENT (WITH SHARP FLINT PEGS)

A GOURD BUCKET AND MAMMOTH-TUSK SPADE
  (FOR BUILDING SAND CAVES)

STRAW SUN HATS

RUSH-WOVEN TOWELS

GRASS-WEAVE FISHING NETS

FIVE BIG SPEARS

THREE CLUBS WITH SPIKES STICKING OUT

The spears and clubs were crucial to guard against any wild animals they met on the way. As an extra precaution, Dirk's parents invited Muzzy's family to come too. There was safety in numbers, they said. Dirk was not pleased about *that*.

Still, when he went to bed that night he could hardly sleep, he was fizzing with so much excitement. The next day, their holiday would begin!

Chapter 6
The seaside

The sun was just peeping above the horizon when they set off on their long journey. They walked and walked until their muscles ached. Every now and then they would be attacked by jackals, lynxes, venomous vipers, and even a horde of fanged water voles, and they would have to fight them off with their clubs and spears. (Even Dirk managed to chase away a small grass snake.) But as Dirk's dad said, what else could you expect on a journey? Nobody got eaten after all, and every night they put up their tent and squashed in together (except for whoever's turn it was to keep watch for jackals and lynxes). Dirk always seemed to end up with Grunk's feet up his nose.

Finally, they saw the sea.

'Be careful!' bellowed Dirk's mum, as the kids raced for the water. 'Watch out for sea monsters!'

Grunk got there first. Dirk dived in and immediately got smacked in the face by an enormous wave. 'Oh Dirk – you gurk!' laughed Muzzy, before performing a graceful swallow dive and surging off through the water, happy as a dolphin.

Dumpa paddled at the edge and grabbed her mum's legs every time a wave came near her.

Faffy stood and gazed moodily over the water.

Then: 'Time to put up the tent!' yelled the grown-ups.

'Time to get some fish!'

'Time to gather some driftwood!'

Soon the fire was burning merrily. Grunk and Muzzy caught some fish (Dirk discovered too late there was a hole in his net) which they roasted on hot stones next to the fire.

After supper, everybody sang songs while Grunk beat time with a couple of stones. The dogs started howling, and that's when they all decided it was time for bed.

It turned out to be pretty much your average seaside holiday.

Dirk's dad met a giant squid and came shooting out of the sea like a stone shot from a sling.

Dumpa had a fight with a giant crab.

Muzzy's mother was so busy putting sun cream all over Muzzy that she forgot to put any on herself, so she got sunburned and couldn't lie down. She spent a whole night standing up on the beach with her feet cooling in a rock pool.

The fathers made two gigantic sand caves and then spent their time arguing about whose cave was biggest. Dirk had a go at building his own, but it kept collapsing. He really didn't see why everyone laughed so much. It wasn't *that* funny.

He also got nipped by a crab, built a raft that got washed away by a wave when his back was turned, and constructed a hut out of branches that fell over when Cross Eye wagged his tail.

Muzzy did not get nipped, and her raft and her hut worked perfectly.

'You just need to be more like *me*, Dirk,' she told him helpfully, at least three times a day.

At least he hadn't been as daft as Grunk, who had decided to try surfing. Unfortunately, Grunk had made his surfboard out of solid granite.

'Have you never heard the expression "sunk like a stone"?' asked his dad as they dragged him out of the sea.

The only real trouble was Faffy. She gathered shells and went swimming. But she spent too much time by herself and Dirk's mother worried about her. She tried to keep an eye on her, especially at mealtimes.

'Try a little grilled fish,' Dirk's mum would say.

'Or a bit of squid.

'Or some tasty crab.

'Octopus is nice.

'Limpets are lovely.

'How about some stewed lugworm?'

Faffy would shake her head and say, 'Just some fried seaweed for me, please.' And then she would leave the fire and wander off to the sea by herself.

One night, Faffy was mooching about on the shore. The grown-ups were all lounging around the fire near the cliffs, and the kids had all been dispatched to bed. The only one awake was Dirk. (Grunk's feet smelled *really* bad.)

After a while, Dirk poked his head out of the tent. He wanted to take a look at the beach in the moonlight (and he also needed a break from Grunk's feet). As it happened, there wasn't much moonlight.

He could barely make out the dark shape of Faffy standing at the water's edge.

'I'm just *so homesick*,' he heard her say in a plaintive voice.

Then he heard her gasp. And the next moment, she had collapsed on to the sand.

Dirk had no doubt what had happened. Faffy had been attacked by a tentacled sea monster, like the one his dad had mentioned. He could actually make it out – a dark mass on the beach. Most likely, it was trying to drag Faffy out to sea so it could consume her.

For a moment, Dirk had a strong temptation to crawl back under the covers and pretend that nothing had happened. But the next moment he was running out of the tent yelling, 'Sea monster! Wake up, everyone!' at the top of his voice.

There was no time to wait for help. Faffy was lying in the shallow water, moaning; dark tentacles were wrapped around her ankles and a sinister, slimy darkness floated on the surface of the sea.

Bravely, Dirk grasped a piece of driftwood and plunged into the sea to fight the monster.

'Geddoff!' he yelled, flailing about him with the wood. 'Leave my cousin alone!'

Almost immediately his foot was caught in a tentacle and he tripped. The monster was wet and slimy and covered in horrible wart-like pustules. Dirk tried to jab its eyes, but couldn't find them. He crawled out of the water on to the sand, still struggling with the monster.

Suddenly, there was a roar of laughter. Dirk looked up to see his entire family, and Muzzy's too, standing watching. His mum was holding a burning branch which lit up the whole beach.

'Why don't you help?' he yelled indignantly.

'Help with what?' they cried. 'You're fighting a pile of seaweed!'

It was true. In the light, Dirk realized that the monster was actually a giant mound of seaweed, swept up by the tide. Faffy had tripped over it, walking on the beach in the dark.

'Really, Dirk,' said Muzzy. 'Even a gurk like you should know the difference between a sea monster and a pile of smelly old seaweed.'

'Gah!' yelled Dirk, throwing a heap of it over her head.

Still, something good came out of it. For the next day, when Dirk's mother passed Faffy her usual plate of fried seaweed, Faffy just shuddered.

'I'm not eating that!' she said. 'I've seen enough seaweed to last a lifetime!' And she tipped it into the nearest rock pool.

'But you'll be hungry,' said Dirk's mum anxiously.

'I'll eat later, or when I get home,' Faffy said.

Dirk's mum looked terribly worried. 'But your home was squashed by a herd of stampeding mammoths!'

'I meant home to Swampy Hollow,' Faffy explained. 'And none of that stewed river fish, if you don't mind. You see, the truth is, Aunty Pumpha, I've never really liked fish or seafood. I didn't say anything because I didn't want to hurt your feelings, but what I'm really longing for is a mammoth kebab.'

So that was the first thing Dirk's mum made for supper when they got back to the village!

Chapter 7
The wild wolves

'You dozy lummock,' Dirk's mum shouted at him. 'Your baby sister pays more attention than you!'

Dirk had been told to help get supper. He had put out a big platter of cold roast marsh fowl in the family eating place, but then he had fallen into a dream in which he was the best hunter in the village. He had just shot down ten marsh fowls with a single arrow, while fighting off an attack from a ferocious bear when ...

'Ecka-ecka-ecka!' screeched Dumpa, pointing.

Dirk turned to see an empty plate. The roast marsh fowl was gone and Cross Eye's tail was vanishing out of the cave entrance!

That's when Dirk's mum called him a 'dozy lummock'. She didn't stop there, either.

'I spent ages cooking that bird, just for you to let the dog get it! There's no more meat in the larder and there won't be any until the next hunting trip. We shall have to eat nuts and berries and swamp lettuce – huh! It's all your fault, Dirk.'

The atmosphere did not improve when the rest

of the family came home. As they chewed on their nuts and berries, plus the odd leaf of swamp lettuce (horrible chewy stuff, with a flavour like ... well ... swamp), they let Dirk know what they thought.

'I've been looking forward to that marsh fowl all day!'

'You mammoth toenail!'

'You bird-brain, you!'

'At least Dumpa did her best.'

'She gave the alarm.'

'Yes, well done, Dumpa.'

Dumpa crowed with delight.

Dirk glowered at his baby sister. *Why do I have to have such a perfect baby sister?* he thought to himself. *She's going to turn out exactly like Muzzy; I just know it*!

Dirk was relieved when the topic of conversation finally moved away from him. His dad told them that a pack of wolves had been seen in the nearby woods. 'They must have come down from the Crinkly Mountains,' he said. 'It's unusual for wolves to visit in summer but there were bad storms on the peaks that may have forced them down. Until they move on, nobody is to go outside of the village alone.'

After dinner, Dirk met Brabbin and Muzzy. They sat outside the cave working on some model animals. It turned out Muzzy and Brabbin had been warned about the wolves, too.

'We might hear them howling later tonight,' speculated Brabbin, rubbing his hands gleefully. 'My dad says to keep well away because they'd eat you as soon as look at you.'

'Nonsense,' Muzzy retorted.

'What do you mean? Everyone knows wolves are ferocious and bloodthirsty!'

'For your information, wolves rarely eat people,' said Muzzy in her superior way. 'If you don't hurt them, they won't hurt you. Like wasps. In fact, sometimes they get on *extremely* well with humans.'

'Rubbish!' scoffed Brabbin. 'Whoever heard of wolves doing anything to humans except biting them?'

'Obviously you know nothing about wolves,' said Muzzy loftily. 'They have very caring natures. For example, wolves sometimes find abandoned human babies and bring them up as their own.'

The two boys looked at her. 'Are you sure?' asked Dirk.

'Of course,' Muzzy replied. 'My granny told me.'

Dirk forgot this conversation until the following day. He came in from a long day of tree-climbing and gathering blackberries, ate his dinner, and then went to find his model antelope. He had been working on it for ages and had almost finished it. But all he found was a little heap of wood, and Dumpa crowing cheerfully as she banged it with her fists.

'Hwah, hwah, hwah!'

'Look what you've done!' Dirk yelled.

'Goo-gah, goo-gah!' said Dumpa, chuckling.

Dirk prised the bits of wood out of her hands, but it was no use – the antelope was beyond repair. Dumpa began to howl.

Faffy said, 'You know, you *really* shouldn't have left it where she could reach it, Dirk.'

(*Thanks a bunch*, thought Dirk.)

'There isn't anywhere she can't reach!' he pointed out.

Dumpa howled louder. Dirk's mum picked up Dumpa and tickled her tummy. 'Did Dirk upset you, Diddums?'

(*Like it's my fault*, thought Dirk.)

'Who's my fluffy little pup!' Dirk's mum cooed. 'Who's my little baby cub then!'

Dirk shook his head in disgust. Still, his mum's words had given him an idea.

When his mum and Faffy had gone back to their own affairs, Dirk grabbed a hide and made up a bundle: Dumpa's favourite bone rattle, her shell bracelet and her stone bottle. Then he put Dumpa into her sling and carried her out of the cave.

'You're going to have a wonderful time, Dumpa,' he told her as he ran towards the deep forest. 'The wolves will look after you, just as if you're their own cub. You'll have lots of wolf cub friends to play with. You'll be able to sleep in a cosy wolf den. You can gnaw on bones and howl at the moon! Won't that be fun?'

Dumpa gurgled happily. Dirk could tell she liked the idea. 'You'll get a lovely holiday and plenty of fresh air, and I'll get a break from having you wreck my stuff! And in a week or so – when I've made another antelope – I'll come and fetch you home.'

The air grew colder; Dumpa felt heavier. Dirk's shoulders ached; so did his feet and his legs.

Just when Dirk felt he couldn't go another step, he heard a howl. Then another. Wolves! And they were getting closer.

Quickly, Dirk laid Dumpa on the ground. Then he ran all the way home.

***

The next morning, Dirk was still half asleep when his mum said, 'Where's Dumpa?'

The family started searching, except for Dirk, who was still struggling to wake up.

'Come on, Dirk,' said his mum. 'You can help too.' Then she narrowed her eyes. 'Wait a moment. Why are you so sleepy? And why won't you look at me? You *know* something about this, don't you?'

'Er ... ' said Dirk. 'Dumpa's just gone to see the wolves, that's all.'

'WHAT!'

Dirk's mother collapsed on to a rock and started fanning herself. Dirk's dad gave an inarticulate bear-like growl. Faffy and Grunk stared at Dirk, mouths agape.

'It's no big deal,' said Dirk quickly. 'We'll go get her back after a week or so. I can remember exactly where I left her ... I think.'

His family looked so horrified that Dirk began to gabble. 'She'll have a wonderful time. She'll gnaw bones and hunt rabbits. The wolves will treat her just like their own cub!'

'What?' screeched Dirk's mum. 'Who told you that?'

'Muzzy,' Dirk said. 'Her granny said so.'

'*Muzzy's granny*! So because of some old tale that Muzzy's granny told her, you think those wolves are going to treat Dumpa like their own cub?'

'Er – well – yes.'

Dirk's mum turned to the rest of the family. 'We need to set out for the woods right now!'

'We'd better bring our spears, and our bows and arrows too,' said Dirk's dad.

They rushed to get ready. *Why had he believed Muzzy?* Dirk wondered, as he searched for his spear.

And why, when she was always right about everything, did this have to be the one time that she was wrong?

***

Dirk's dad charged out of the cave entrance, pursued by the rest of the family. Suddenly, he stopped short, and the rest of the family went *thump*, *bang*, *clump* into the back of him.

'Ouch!'

'Watch where you're going!'

'I've stubbed my toe!'

But then they saw why he had stopped. Lying in the grass was a bundle. The bundle was making a gurgling noise.

'Dumpa!' they all yelled, crowding in to see. There was their baby, beaming happily at them.

'She must have crawled all the way home!' cried Dirk's mum delightedly.

The rest of the family went inside with Dumpa, but Dirk stayed where he was. He reckoned his parents would forgive him for taking his little sister to the wolves ... eventually. But they might need some time to get over it first!

He was still sitting there, not entirely sure what to do, when he heard a sound: a kind of rustling.

He looked up and was astonished to see, sticking out of the bushes opposite him, a pair of grey ears. The ears twitched, and some of the leaves parted, and then a long grey snout emerged, topped by a pair of gleaming, grey eyes.

It was a wolf.

Dirk sat, frozen to the rock. He could not even shout for help.

The wolf padded forward and gazed deep into Dirk's eyes, and at that moment Dirk felt that it was telling him all kinds of amazing things about the dark woods, the deep caves in the mountains, and the long nights on the snow-capped peaks.

'You brought Dumpa back, didn't you?' asked Dirk at last.

The wolf seemed to nod.

'Thank you,' Dirk whispered.

The wolf turned back into the undergrowth, but instead of leaving, it picked up something in its mouth and brought it over to Dirk. It dropped the thing on the grass, and after a surprised moment Dirk realized it was a wolf cub.

The wolf raised its paw and pointed first at the cub, and then at Dirk.

Dirk blinked. 'You want me to take the wolf cub and look after it?'

The wolf nodded.

'But I can't do that!' Dirk protested. 'I'm a boy!'

The wolf gave a low growl deep in its throat. Its eyes narrowed and gazed fixedly into Dirk's. Once again, it seemed to be conveying some kind of message.

This wolf cub has no parents, it seemed to say. *It is too small to make it back to the mountains. Besides, you owe me one, cave boy*!

It is never wise to argue with a creature that has bigger teeth than you.

Dirk looked down at the cub. It was small, but looked healthy and cheerful. It put its head on one side and fixed its gaze on Dirk.

'All right,' Dirk gulped. 'I'll do it.'

He looked up, but the wolf had already left to rejoin its pack.

Dirk's parents were so pleased to get Dumpa back that they didn't shout at Dirk *that* much – just most of the morning and half the afternoon. When they found out about the wolf cub, they did some more shouting. But in the end they had to admit that Dirk was right: they *did* owe the wolves a favour for bringing Dumpa back home.

Dirk still felt bad about what he'd done, though. Why had he put his sister in danger?

Dirk's dad must have realized how he was feeling. 'Don't feel too badly, son,' he said late that night, when Dirk was curled up in bed with the wolf cub on his feet. 'I remember how my little brother used to drive me crazy when I was growing up. I often wished some wild animals would come and eat *him*.'

'I bet you never gave him to the wolves, though, did you?' asked Dirk.

'Certainly not,' said Dirk's dad. 'I'd have given him to the bears!'

Chapter 8
Tickles

Dirk spent a lot of time thinking of names for his new wolf cub. It was very important that she should have a really impressive, ferocious-sounding name. He decided on The Untamable, the Tyrannical, Terror-Tooth the First!

Only everyone called her Tickles.

Tickles was very good-tempered for a wolf. She loved following Dirk around, having her tummy tickled and cuddling up on his bed at night. Dirk spent a lot of time attempting to persuade her to be a bit more ferocious, but he usually ended up feeding her scraps or letting her climb into his lap.

Training wolf cubs is not easy. Tickles never saw why she should 'Fetch' or 'Heel' or 'Lie Down' just because that was what Dirk said.

'I wish you'd *focus* more,' Dirk told her, when, instead of running after a stick when he yelled 'Fetch', she decided to sit down and have a good scratch. 'Still,' he added quickly, 'I suppose this is a bit like school for you and, believe me, school isn't everything. I bet you're a fearsome hunter. We'll go out tomorrow and see how you do.'

So the next morning they got up early and set off before anyone could ask where they were going.

It wasn't long before a rabbit bolted out of the undergrowth.

'Tickles!' yelled Dirk excitedly. 'Look! Prey! Chase! Kill!' Tickles just gaped.

So Dirk bounded after the rabbit, to give her the idea.

When he turned around, Tickles had disappeared. He found her hiding behind a tree.

'You're a *wolf*,' he said disgustedly. 'You're not supposed to be scared of rabbits!' Tickles just sat and meekly rubbed her paw over her nose. She was obviously seriously lacking in bloodlust.

Still, Dirk did not give up.

He encouraged Tickles to chase a squirrel. Tickles ran the opposite way.

So Dirk found her a shrew to hunt.

She sat down and looked confused.

So *then* Dirk found her a mouse. Tickles squeaked and quivered nervously.

'Oh, Tickles!' Dirk said despairingly. 'I give up!' Tickles wandered off through the trees, and a few minutes later, to Dirk's astonishment, he saw her running away with something brown and furry in her mouth. She had caught something after all!

'Oh, Tickles!' he yelled, bursting with pride. 'Well done!'

Then, from the river, there came a bellow of rage. 'She's run off with my bathrobe!'

It was Chief Windabag.

It took ages to catch Tickles and return the bathrobe to a very chilly and bad-tempered Chief Windabag. Afterwards, as they walked back to the village, Dirk gave Tickles a serious talking-to.

'Listen, Tickles, you mustn't steal and you *must* hunt. It's what wolves do, if they want to eat. You don't want to starve, do you?' Tickles looked mischievously at Dirk. She even seemed to wink.

'That's not the right attitude,' said Dirk crossly. 'You've got to take this seriously!' Tickles tossed her head.

'Oh, so you're not bothered, are you? Well, I'm

not giving you anything until you prove you can find food.'

Tickles galloped off. Dirk blinked. A few minutes later Tickles reappeared, and this time she had something in her mouth.

Dirk stared. 'What's that you've got? Have you actually caught something? You have! Good wolf! Oh – wait a minute ... ' Tickles had caught something all right – a haunch of venison off the fire. In fact, she had nabbed Chief Windabag's supper.

'Mum and Dad are *really* cross,' Brabbin told Dirk later that day. 'All Dad had for his meal was swamp lettuce, and he hates swamp lettuce. He wants you to come before the Village Council tomorrow. He said to bring "that animal", too.'

The Village Council was made up of some of the wisest people in Swampy Hollow – plus Chief Windabag. Dirk didn't relish being summoned before it. He did not think it was a good sign.

He was right.

'It has come to my attention,' Chief Windabag announced to the rest of the Council, 'that certain people have brought Unsuitable Animals into

the village. And by Unsuitable Animals I mean –
WOLVES.'

The rest of the Council gasped and turned to
stare at Dirk and Tickles. They gasped even
though they all knew Tickles perfectly well and
had seen her every day since her arrival. This is
simply the effect that the word 'WOLVES'
usually has.

'Well,' said Chief Windabag. 'What have you
got to say?'

'Tickles doesn't do any harm,' said Dirk in a
small voice.

'That's not what I've heard,' said Chief Windabag.
'I've heard she steals valuable cuts of meat that
would have made a well-deserved dinner for certain
esteemed and respected members of this village.'

'All dogs do that kind of thing,' said Dirk.

'No, they don't,' said Chief Windabag. 'Anyway,
she's not a dog, she's a wolf, and wolves are
dangerous. What about when she's full-grown?
We don't want to find she's eaten someone when
we weren't looking.'

The rest of the Council nodded.

'So that's decided,' said Chief Windabag. 'Unless

anybody can see a good reason why this wolf cub should not be banished from the village … '

'Wait!' said Dirk quickly.

'Well?'

Dirk tried desperately to think of a reason why Tickles should not be sent away, when suddenly he had a flash of inspiration. 'I think we should ask Old Wrinkly One! Let's see what she decides.'

Old Wrinkly One was the oldest person in Swampy Hollow. She was completely blind and almost deaf and could not walk and was more crinkled than a dried-up leaf at the end of autumn. She was also, without doubt, the wisest person in Swampy Hollow. All the villagers respected her and hoped that one day they would be as old and wise and wrinkly as she was.

'Humph,' said Chief Windabag. He couldn't really refuse to ask the wisest person in the village for her opinion. So off they went to seek her out.

Old Wrinkly One was sitting in her hut, humming to herself. She listened as Chief Windabag explained the situation, bellowing at the top of his voice. Then she went into a kind of trance.

A bit later (just as Dirk was beginning to wonder if she had fallen asleep) she gave a start, then pointed at Tickles and said in a quavering voice: 'All the puppies in the village must do a test when they reach a certain age, is that not so?'

'Yes,' everyone agreed.

'Then this animal must do the test also. According to how she performs ... '

'Yes?' asked Chief Windabag.

' ... the right decision will be clear!'

Dirk was dismayed. The test the puppies did was an obedience test. He would have to show that Tickles could obey commands such as 'Heel', 'Fetch' and 'Lie Down'. So far, Tickles could do none of those things.

He told Brabbin and Muzzy his problem.

'Don't worry,' said Muzzy. 'We'll embark on a strict training regime!'

'Yes, we'll sort it,' Brabbin said.

They tried the following three methods:

1. Reward. When Tickles did as she was told, she was rewarded with a piece of meat. The trouble was Tickles never did what she was told.

2. Punishment. When Tickles did *not* do as she was told, Dirk said 'bad wolf', or made her sleep outside the cave. The trouble was Tickles just wagged her tail when she was told off, and when left outside the cave, she just howled until she was let in again.

3. Copying. Dirk used Cross Eye the dog to show

Tickles how things should be done. Then he praised Cross Eye. The trouble was Tickles did not care what Cross Eye did and usually made off before Dirk could start praising anybody.

***

The day of the test arrived all too soon. The puppies and their owners gathered in an open space in the middle of Swampy Hollow and, as it was a nice day, most of the villagers came to watch. Even Old Wrinkly One was there.

Dirk was nervous but hopeful. Tickles had been doing slightly better in her training recently. Only *then* he heard what the onlookers were saying.

'Wolves are dangerous!'

'I mean, look at its claws!'

'Look at its snout!'

'Look at its *teeth*!'

The test began. Dirk hurled his stick across the grass and yelled at the top of his voice, 'Fetch!' Tickles was watching all the other dogs. She was much more interested in them than in paying attention to Dirk. And while she was watching, she amused herself by balancing on three legs.

So when Dirk yelled 'Fetch!' again Tickles got such a surprise she fell over. The whole village erupted with laughter. Tickles just picked herself up and grinned at everyone, with her mischievous wolf grin.

Things deteriorated fast. When Tickles was supposed to 'Come!' she sat and had a good scratch instead. When she was supposed to 'Sit!' she caught sight of Dumpa and went running off to play. When she was supposed to 'Lie Down!' she lay on her back with her tummy in the air and waved her legs.

The villagers of Swampy Hollow laughed uproariously. Some of them collapsed on to the ground, they were laughing so hard. Some of them were actually weeping with laughter.

Dirk turned to Chief Windabag.

'All right, so she's failed the test, but listen to me! If you banish Tickles then I'll go too!'

Chief Windabag pursed his lips.

But before he could say anything, the rest of the villagers began to shout out.

'You can't send her away!'

'You can see she wouldn't hurt a mouse!'

'She may be a wolf, but she's softer than any dog!'

The whole village was united. Chief Windabag had no choice but to relent. As for Old Wrinkly One – she just smiled mysteriously to herself, as if this were exactly what she had expected all along.

Chapter 9
Harumpha

One fine morning, Dirk, Brabbin and Muzzy were playing on the scree heap at one end of the village. The scree heap was a huge pile of all the stone chippings from the tools that the village had made over the years. It was fun to clamber on to the top then career down at full pelt, digging your heels into the shingly stones.

Brabbin, especially, loved going really fast. 'Whoo hoo!' he yelled.

When Dirk reached the bottom, Tickles would be waiting and would rush round, jumping up and wagging her tail.

They were all having a rest, while Muzzy gave the boys tips for braking in scree, when suddenly a little man with a long beard shot out of one of the huts close by.

'Eubeeka!' he yelled, jumping up and down with excitement.

The little man was called Harumpha. He was something of an outsider in the village, who never went hunting or gathering, but instead stayed home, inventing things. The villagers put up with this because sometimes the things Harumpha invented were quite useful. For example, he had made foot scrapers out of animal bone, and now every cave and hut in the village had its own foot scraper proudly displayed outside the entrance, and when people got home they could scrape all the mud and swamp off their feet before going inside. They admitted that the "chimbley" he had invented to let the smoke from the cooking fires escape from the caves and huts (so that everybody didn't have to sit around coughing, or stink of smoke) was quite a good idea too. But the villagers still grumbled because often the things Harumpha invented weren't useful at all. The stupidest invention, they all agreed, was a round, flat disc which he called a "wheel". What a pointless waste of time that was!

'What does "eubeeka" mean, Harumpha?' asked Muzzy.

'It's a new expression I just invented,' said Harumpha. 'It means: I've just made a wonderful new invention!'

'What invention?' asked Dirk.

'Go and fetch the rest of the village!' cried Harumpha. So they did.

'Now then,' said Chief Windabag when everybody had assembled. 'What is this all about, Harumpha?'

Harumpha rushed into his hut and came back, proudly bearing his new invention. He laid it down in front of them. It certainly didn't look anything special.

'What on earth is it?' demanded Dirk's mum.

'It is my marvellous new invention,' declared Harumpha proudly. 'I made it by twisting vines together according to my special, secret, Harumpha method! I call it – rope!'

The villagers all looked at the new invention more closely and then they started shouting very rude things at Harumpha.

'What a load of rubbish!'

'You dragged us away from our work for this?'

'Stupid old rope!'

'It's even worse than the wheel!'

Then they all marched off back to their homes.

'Never mind, Harumpha,' said Dirk. 'I'm sure it must be good for *something*.'

'We can stay and help you with it, if you like,' said Muzzy.

Harumpha just grunted and marched into his hut. Dirk, Muzzy and Brabbin stayed in Harumpha's yard, trying to think of things to do with the rope, and fiddling around with all the other fascinating pieces of junk (or possibly inventions) that he had left lying around.

Brabbin soon got bored and went back to the scree slope, but Dirk picked up some bits of rock and some discarded wheels and began playing with them. He felt sorry for Harumpha and wanted to help. He knew how it felt when people said you were no good.

'Right,' said Muzzy eventually. 'Who wants to see the things I've invented to do with rope?'

Neither Dirk or Brabbin were very keen, but Muzzy insisted, so Dirk put down the contraption he had made and Brabbin slid down the scree to join them.

'Number One: When you're fishing with a spear, you can attach the rope to one end so it doesn't get lost.

'Number Two: You can tie your boat to the shore with the rope, so it doesn't get lost.

'Number Three: You can tie the rope around your dog's neck so he or she doesn't get lost.'

'Worra-worra-worra!' howled Tickles indignantly.

'But Tickles isn't a dog, she's a wolf, and she never does get lost,' Dirk protested.

'All right, so you can tie it around her neck so she doesn't go roaming about and doing her business right outside next door's cave,' said Muzzy, giving Tickles a hard look.

Muzzy and Dirk were so busy arguing that they hadn't been paying attention to Brabbin. He had gone to look at Dirk's inventions. Suddenly he yelled, 'Eubeeka!'

They turned and stared at him. 'What is it?'

'Look what *I* invented!' yelled Brabbin. He was holding up a slab of stone. Four of the little discs that Harumpha called "wheels" were attached to the bottom.

'Hey, *I* made that,' said Dirk. But nobody paid any attention to him.

'Just watch!' yelled Brabbin. Then he ran to the path that led to the main village. This path was made of rock, and it had been worn smooth by so many feet treading on it over the years.

Brabbin put down the slab of stone, leaped on top and ...

'Wheeeeeeee!' He went rolling off down the path.

'Hey, but it was me who attached the wheels!' yelled Dirk. 'I thought of it!'

But nobody was paying any attention. All the children in the village, and some of the grown-ups too, were running out to look at Brabbin and his wonderful new invention.

'Let me have a go!'

'It's so fast!'

'What do you call it?'

Brabbin, very pleased with himself, thought for a moment. 'I'm calling it the slateboard!'

Soon, slateboards were all the craze in Swampy Hollow. Everybody (at least those below a certain age) wanted one. Everybody went rummaging for long, smooth slabs of slate, and everyone was chipping away at little round discs of stone to make wheels. And everybody was congratulating Brabbin on his wonderful idea.

'But it was me who attached the wheels, and it was Harumpha who invented them!' Dirk complained. He couldn't believe that he'd actually done something good and that Brabbin was getting all the credit.

'Now you know how *I* feel,' Muzzy told him. 'Nobody cares about all the wonderful things I've found to do with rope, either.'

Grunk and his friends were especially keen on this new craze. They would go down each day to a place by the river where there were lots of big boulders and do all kinds of jumps and somersaults on their new slateboards.

Brabbin had another idea, too. He attached a tall piece of wood to the front of the slateboard and gave it to some of the younger children. He called it a "slooter". Dumpa had a little one, and she would pester Dirk until he pushed her along.

Dirk felt really fed up, but eventually he decided the only thing to do was to come up with an even *better* invention. He spent every day at Harumpha's yard, messing around, and struggling to invent something.

At last he thought he had done it.

'Just look at this!' he told his family that evening. He sat Tickles down and gave her a bone to gnaw. Then he moved a few steps away and took a coil of rope from around his waist. It had a loop on one end.

'Are you all watching?'

'Get on with it!' they said.

Dirk waved the rope round and round his head, and got ready to throw ...

Dumpa pointed at Tickles. 'Ulf!' she said, and began to chuckle.

'Oh, clever Dumpa!' cried Dirk's mum. 'Ulf! It's her first word!'

'Ulf's not a word,' said Dad.

'It means "wolf", of course,' said Mum.

'How do you know?' Faffy asked. 'It might mean something completely different.'

'Like what?'

'Like, "What's that strange thing Dirk is waving around his head?"'

'But ... ' Dirk had got very red in the face. 'Look, can you all pay attention to me for once?'

He threw the rope, but all the squabbling had put him off, and instead of the loop going round Tickles's head, like he had intended, it fell short. His family weren't impressed.

'And what's the point of that, exactly?'

'Well, you see, I've tied it with a special type of knot. It's supposed to go round Tickles's head and tighten. It's called a Catch-A-Roo. I thought we could use it for catching deer when we're hunting.'

'I'd like to see you get close enough to get that

thing round a deer's head,' his dad scoffed. 'It would hear you coming right from the other side of the wood!'

'Lass-oo, lass-oo!' yelled Dumpa, who couldn't manage Catch-A-Roo.

'Yeah, silly old lasso,' said Grunk.

Dirk stalked off. Nobody appreciated him and his brilliant ideas! Now he knew how Harumpha felt!

However, when he tried hunting with his new lasso he had to admit his dad was right. The deer in the woods would just wait until he was a few steps away, and then, before Dirk could even throw his rope, they would go bounding off through the trees.

'I'll just have to think again,' he told Tickles.

Eventually he had an idea: he would hide in a tree holding the end of the rope, with the lasso loop lying on the ground below. When an unsuspecting animal wandered into the loop, the lasso would pull tight and capture the animal.

He sat in the tree waiting patiently, but after a while he drifted into a daydream and wasn't really paying attention when:

'AAAAAAAAAAAHHHHH!'

There was a huge shout and the rope tightened. Dirk almost fell out of the tree. 'It's worked!' he yelled. Tickles started to howl: 'Worra-worra-worra!' Of course, everyone within earshot came running to see what had happened.

What they saw was Chief Windabag, suspended upside down from the tree, with his foot caught in Dirk's rope.

'Get me down at once!' bellowed Chief Windabag, his face bright scarlet.

The villagers collapsed with laughter. But Chief Windabag did not see the funny side.

At first he wanted to banish Dirk to the Crinkly Mountains ('Let's see what the wolves think of your new invention!') but he calmed down a little after Dirk's friends pleaded on his behalf.

'Please don't send him away, Dad,' Brabbin begged. 'Poor old Dirk – he's just feeling bad because *I* invented the slateboard and he didn't. It's not *his* fault his new invention is so rubbish.'

'Yes,' Muzzy agreed. 'It's hard having friends as brilliant as us, when you're a bit useless like Dirk.'

'Thanks for that,' muttered Dirk.

'Oh, very well!' puffed Chief Windabag. 'I expect the wolves would send him straight back anyway. But I am seriously angry, Dirk! I am fed up with your troublesome ways! Go to your cave and stay there until I decide on your punishment!'

Chapter 10
Help!

That night Dirk couldn't sleep. It wasn't fair. His lasso animal trap would have been wonderful, he knew – if only Chief Windabag hadn't come along and put his foot in it! Dirk crept out of bed and went to sit in the mouth of the cave, next to the embers of the dying fire.

There wasn't much to see. The villagers were asleep and the caves and huts were dark; the woods were even darker. All Dirk could hear was the occasional squeak of a bat or the deep-throated croak of a swamp toad.

Here I am, he thought, *No Good Dirk, sitting all alone in the dark on a cold, hard rock, with my hands and feet going numb.*

After a long while, Dirk realized something was moving in the undergrowth close by. At first he didn't pay it much attention, but then he began to squint a little, trying to work out what it was.

It looks quite big, he thought. *Bigger than a squirrel or a rat. Maybe it's that wolf come back. Maybe it's come to take Tickles away.*

This was such a terrible thought that Dirk got up

and advanced towards the undergrowth, clutching a piece of firewood in his hand. He wasn't about to give Tickles back. No way! He'd make that plain! And if the wolf wanted to argue ... if it wanted to argue ... well, Dirk would ... he would ... well, he'd run away very fast, that's what he would do!

He was just wondering if it might not be better to run away now, *before* the wolf had a chance to argue, when he heard something.

I didn't know wolves could purr, thought Dirk. Just then the leaves on the nearest tree moved a little, maybe because of a slight breeze – or maybe because of something breathing. That was when Dirk saw an eye.

It was a bright, amber-coloured eye. And it was gazing down at Dirk.

Owls have amber eyes, thought Dirk, but something told him this was not an owl. For one thing, owls don't purr.

Then he saw something else, dangling from the same tree. It was a tail. A yellow tail with black spots.

That's when Dirk felt as if all the blood in his veins had turned to ice and a whole family of bouncing bullfrogs had taken up residence in his stomach.

Because now he knew what it was that was watching him from that tree.

A Snaggle-Toothed Swamp Cat.

All his life, Dirk had heard tales of the deadly Snaggle-Toothed Swamp Cat. Everyone knew it was the most fearsome animal to be found anywhere in wood, swamp or mountain, but none of the villagers had ever met one. Kylar Spear Arm's grandfather had once had an epic battle with a Snaggle-Toothed Swamp Cat and escaped (just about) to tell the tale, but nobody had seen one in the flesh since then. Many villagers had hoped that the Snaggle-Toothed Swamp Cat – if it still existed – had gone to live far, far away from Swampy Hollow and would never come back.

Only now it had.

Dirk took a step back. Then another. He thought he could hear a slight hissing sound emanating from the beast.

'Nice kitty,' he said. Then he leaped back into the cave.

Just in time. The Snaggle-Toothed Swamp Cat did not like being called 'nice kitty'. It pounced. As Dirk burst into the cave and scuttled backwards at top speed, he could hear it land on the ground outside and hiss with indignation at finding its prey gone.

Dirk kicked at the half-dead fire and it started to flare up again.

Dirk knew wild animals were unnerved by fire. Sure enough, when he poked his head out of the cave, the Swamp Cat was gone. But he knew it would not have gone far.

'Wake up!' bawled Dirk at the top of his voice. He grabbed a spear and banged it against the rocky wall of the cave. CLUMP! CLUMP! CLUMP!

'Wake up!' he yelled again. 'Snaggle-Toothed Swamp Cat on the loose!'

'What are you talking about, Dirk?' murmured his mum sleepily, while Tickles bounced around the cave making worra-worra noises.

'You've had a nightmare, that's what it is,' said his dad, turning over and pulling the covers over his head.

Faffy and Grunk didn't even seem to have woken up, and Dumpa was sucking her toes. Dirk left them to it, and with Tickles at his side, ran into the village.

'Wake up! Swamp Cat alert, Swamp Cat alert!' he yelled.

Eventually the villagers, yawning and bleary-eyed, came wandering out of their caves and huts and into the middle of the village.

'What's going on?'

'Must be a mammoth stampede.'

'Or an enraged porcupine!'

'Maybe it's a bristly bear from the forest.'

'Perhaps there's a flood.'

'Or a fire.'

'Or a landslide.'

'Or a flood *and* a fire *and* a landslide ... '

Eventually they realized that Dirk was the source of the alarm. Chief Windabag put his hands on his hips and glared at him. 'Now then, Dirk, what's going on? I thought I told you to stay in your cave until I said otherwise.'

'But you don't understand,' said Dirk. 'There's a Snaggle-Toothed Swamp Cat on the loose.'

The villagers looked at him, then fell about laughing.

'A Snaggle-Toothed Swamp Cat!'

'A little wildcat more likely.'

'Or maybe a squirrel.'

'Snaggle-Toothed Swamp Cat! He must think we were born yesterday.'

Somebody elbowed their way to the front of the crowd. 'Don't you talk about Dirk like that! If he says he saw a Snaggle-Toothed Swamp Cat, then that's what he saw!' It was Dirk's mum, dragging his dad alongside her.

'OW – yes, that's right,' said Dirk's dad, who had just been elbowed in the ribs by Dirk's mum.

'Yerrr,' grunted Grunk, joining them.

'Dirk's very reliable,' put in Faffy.

Dirk was touched (not to mention astonished) that his family were defending him, but the rest of the villagers weren't impressed.

'Reliable? Like that time he saw a sea monster that turned out to be a heap of seaweed? Like the time he fell into a ditch on a mammoth hunt? That kind of reliable? Yes, we've all heard about it.'

'Yes, enough of this nonsense!' Chief Windabag wagged his finger. 'It's just the kind of rubbishy, attention-seeking, fantastical, ridiculous—'

'GROWLLLLLLLLLLL!'

Everyone froze.

'Well, I wonder if we all aren't just hearing things,' began Chief Windabag, with a nervous laugh.

'GROWWWWWWLLLL!' went the Snaggle-Toothed Swamp Cat again, just in case there should be any doubt.

'Fetch the spears!' yelled Kylar Spear Arm. 'And stick together!' He thumped Dirk on the back and said, 'Good job, Dirk! You've probably saved us from waking up to find we're about to become a Swamp Cat's breakfast!'

What the villagers of Swampy Hollow *should* have done next was to obey Kylar Spear Arm and run, in an orderly manner, to fetch their weapons, and then to assemble in the centre of the village, where they could have lit a large bonfire to keep the Swamp Cat away. This was the Emergency Procedure in the Case of a Wild Animal Attack, and Chief Windabag had often reminded them of it, at length, in his after-dinner speech at village special occasions. The trouble was that the villagers never paid much attention to Chief Windabag's speeches, and they were so bored with hearing him droning on and on about Emergency Procedures in particular, that they had long ago stopped listening to what the procedures actually were.

Instead, they panicked. In fact, one of the worst panickers was Chief Windabag himself, who just ran round in circles, yelling, 'Fire! Flood! Wild hedgehogs!' at the top of his voice. The rest of the villagers were doing much the same thing, and the very few who had kept their heads (like Kylar Spear Arm) couldn't get the others to do anything sensible.

'Fetch the spears!' Kylar yelled repeatedly, as they ran in and out of their homes, but instead of bringing spears they brought things like their favourite bead necklace that their granny gave them, or a bit of honeycomb that they were saving for a special occasion, or in the case of the younger villagers, their new slateboards. Eventually somebody yelled, 'Head for the woods!' and like a herd of stampeding mammoths, they all clattered off in that direction.

Dirk found himself running next to Muzzy. 'Why are we running towards the woods?' he panted. 'I mean, isn't the Swamp Cat more likely to be hiding there?'

'I don't know why *you're* running to the woods,' gasped Muzzy, 'but I know why *I'm* running there.'

'Why?'

'Because I'm very good at climbing trees!'

As Dirk was rubbish at climbing trees, he did not find that much comfort. In fact, when they finally arrived in the woods, he was one of the last to hoist himself into the branches. He couldn't get a good grip and kept sliding back down the trunk. Luckily, the last time this happened, something stopped Dirk falling to the ground, and he found that he still had his coil of rope attached to his back and it had caught on a bit of branch. So then he was able to scramble up the tree to safety.

PHEW! he thought. *That was close.* All he had to do now was to sit tight and wait for the creature to go. It wouldn't be able to get at him, after all ... it wasn't as if Swamp Cats could climb trees.

EEK! Dirk felt his veins freezing up and his stomach filling with bullfrogs *all over again.*

Of course Swamp Cats could climb trees. Why, the first time he had set eyes on the Snaggle-Toothed Swamp Cat, it had been *sitting in a tree.* Now here was the whole of Swampy Hollow, sitting in trees, waiting for the dreaded cat to appear.

Yikes!

For a while they all just sat there. As time went on, and the creature did not appear, Dirk cheered up a bit. Brabbin was in the same tree as him, so they were able to keep each other company. They agreed things might be better than they first appeared, for the following reasons:

1. Even though Swamp Cats can climb trees, the Swamp Cat might not feel in a climbing sort of mood.

2. Even if it were in a climbing mood, the Swamp Cat might not see them because they would be hidden by the leaves.

3. Even if it were in a climbing sort of mood and the Swamp Cat did see them, it couldn't possibly eat *all* the villagers, because its stomach wasn't big enough. So Dirk and Brabbin still had a pretty good chance of escaping.

Only then something happened that smashed this dream.

'Worra-worra-worra-worra!'

Tickles had followed Dirk's scent all the way from the village, and now she was sitting under his tree, howling.

'Stop her!' yelped Brabbin. 'The Swamp Cat's sure to hear and when it does, it will come straight to our tree!'

Dirk leaned over the branch. 'Tickles – quiet!' he whispered. But Tickles had never shown much sign of being an obedient wolf, and she continued howling.

One part of Dirk was really pleased that Tickles cared enough to follow him and sit under his tree.

The other (larger) part thought that this wouldn't be much comfort when the Swamp Cat turned up.

Still, there was no sign of it yet. Perhaps it had gone off in the direction of Boggy Dell. Perhaps it was so busy eating Boggers that it would forget all about the Swampy Hollow villagers. Dirk was able to think this comforting thought for all of two minutes until ...

'GRRRRRRRROWLLLL!'

The Snaggle-Toothed Swamp Cat had arrived!

Chapter 11
Trapped!

'Stay still,' whispered Brabbin, who was trembling like a leaf. 'If we don't make a sound maybe it won't notice us!'

There was just one problem with this idea, Dirk realized. Even if the Swamp Cat hadn't yet noticed the boys, it had definitely noticed Tickles. In fact, it was staring right at her, and while Dirk watched, it licked its lips.

'Run, Tickles!' hissed Dirk. But Tickles just laid her ears back and wagged her tail. Then, finally, she seemed to become aware of a presence behind her. She turned around and saw the Swamp Cat.

But Tickles still didn't run. Instead, she backed up against the trunk of the tree and bared her teeth at the Swamp Cat.

'What's she doing?' muttered Brabbin.

'She's defending us,' said Dirk proudly.

But then he realized how hopeless it was. Why, oh why, had Tickles chosen this moment, of all moments, to act like a fierce, brave wolf? Even if she had been full-grown, she wouldn't have had much chance against a Snaggle-Toothed Swamp Cat. As it was, she was likely to be devoured any second.

'I've got to save her!' he told Brabbin.

'How?' asked Brabbin.

Dirk grabbed the coil of rope from his back. He waved it over his head and sent the looped end towards the Swamp Cat. He planned to drop it over its head.

He missed.

He threw again.

He missed again.

He threw again.

He missed again.

Still, at least the Swamp Cat wasn't attacking Tickles. It was too puzzled about what Dirk was doing.

'I know – try aiming for that tree trunk there,' Brabbin suggested, pointing.

'But I don't want to catch the tree trunk!'

'Just do it!'

So Dirk did. To his annoyance, Brabbin was right – now that he wasn't aiming for the Swamp Cat, the rope went straight for it and would have caught it easily ... except that at the last moment the creature moved towards the tree.

'Oh, bother,' said Dirk.

By now, the Swamp Cat had lost interest in Dirk's rope and was heading towards Tickles. It was crouched down low, its tail swishing, as it prepared to pounce.

There was only one thing to do, so Dirk did it. He jumped down from his tree.

There was a gasp from the villagers in the surrounding trees when they saw what Dirk was doing. 'Get back!' they yelled, but Dirk was impervious to their cries.

He waved his arms at the terrible beast.

'Hey, you oversized moggy! You big scaredy-cat! Look at me!'

Dirk threw the rope again. It bounced off the Swamp Cat's nose! He kept throwing the rope and kept missing. Still, something *was* happening. The Swamp Cat wasn't trying to pounce. It was just sitting there, goggling at him.

The truth was that the waving rope was hypnotizing the creature. As it followed the rope's

snake-like movements with its eyes, the Swamp Cat
grew more and more dazed.

'That's brilliant, Dirk!' cried Brabbin
encouragingly. 'All you have to do is keep throwing!'

'But I can't do this forever!' yelled Dirk. His arms
ached excruciatingly.

Zoooooom! Something swooped across the grass
towards Dirk. For a horrible moment he thought
it might be another Swamp Cat, but it was Muzzy.
She was moving so fast because she was on
her slateboard.

'Don't worry, Dirk, you're not alone – oof!'
Muzzy's slateboard hit a bit of twig and she fell off.
Luckily the Swamp Cat was still entranced by the
swinging action of Dirk's rope.

Muzzy scrambled to her feet. 'I'm here to help!'

'Me too!' It was Grunk, on his slateboard. Faffy
was with him.

'What shall we do?' asked Muzzy.

Dirk (still swinging his rope) thought it would
be nice if someone who *wasn't* him had an idea for a
change, but there didn't seem much point saying so.
And then he did have an idea.

'Listen to me,' he yelled (still swinging the rope).

This was what they did ...

Muzzy, Grunk and Faffy got back on their
slateboards, and each took hold of the rope. Then
they slated round and round the Swamp Cat as
fast as they could. They were going too fast for
it to catch them, and as they slated, the rope
went round and round the beast until it was all
wrapped up.

'Hooray!' yelled Brabbin, jumping down from the
tree. 'You did it!'

'Hooray!' yelled Grunk, Faffy, Muzzy and Dirk.

'Worra-worra-worra!' went Tickles.

The rest of the villagers heard them yelling and reckoned either the Swamp Cat had been defeated, or else it was busy eating someone, and that either way it must be safe to come down. So they did. When they found the Swamp Cat all wrapped up in the rope, they were very impressed.

'We need to get rid of this animal!' said Chief Windabag, though he didn't seem to have any clue about how to do it.

Luckily, Dirk and his friends had yet another good idea.

It's not that easy, tugging along a ferocious Swamp Cat wrapped up in rope and balanced on slateboards, but with the whole village helping they managed it. The younger children cleared a smooth path in front of them, and everyone else tugged or pushed (or bossed everyone else), while all the village dogs barked and Tickles raced around going, 'Worra-worra-worra.'

They set the Swamp Cat down a long, long way from Swampy Hollow.

'How are we going to stop the creature coming after us?' someone asked.

It was Muzzy who knew the answer. 'If it's very dizzy, then it won't be able to come after any of us.'

So, with the Swamp Cat snarling and spitting, they grabbed hold of one end of the rope. Then they spun the creature round, as fast as they possibly could ... until the rope had unwound. And then they ran as fast as they could back in the direction of Swampy Hollow.

As they ran, they heard the most enormous ROAAAAAARRRR! But they never saw the Swamp Cat again.

***

A few weeks later (when they were absolutely certain the Swamp Cat wasn't coming back) they held a special feast to celebrate their Great Escape. They gorged themselves on roast grasshoppers and stewed mud worms and eel pie and mammoth kebabs and swamp frog on sticks, and when Chief Windabag insisted on making one of his long speeches, nobody really minded. Anyway, they were too full to object.

Dirk was too busy tickling Tickles, and passing her treats, to listen. So he was taken by surprise when

Chief Windabag called him up to present him with the Order of the Pointy Flint.

'I give you this, Dirk,' Chief Windabag announced, 'the highest honour in Swampy Hollow, in recognition of your extreme courage and ingenuity! Thanks to you, Swampy Hollow escaped unscathed from the threat of the dreaded Snaggle-Toothed Swamp Cat. Your name will long be mentioned with reverence and respect, when we recall the daring deeds of great heroes such as Ugbert Big Knuckle or Wallump Wallop Chin. Their names will be no more glorious and esteemed than that of our very own Dirk. No longer *No Good Dirk* but *Dirk Who Turned Out To Be Pretty Good After All*!'

At that, everyone stopped feasting and burping and scratching their chins and rubbing their tummies long enough to give a big cheer.

Brabbin got to his feet. 'I think you should all know,' he said, 'it was Dirk who invented the slateboard. All I did was make it go.'

They cheered louder than ever. Dirk felt so happy he could burst. It was the proudest day of his life!

He went back to where Muzzy and Brabbin were sitting.

'I could never have done it without you,' he said.

'Well, of course,' said Muzzy.

'Goes without saying,' said Brabbin.

'Worra-worra-worra!' went Tickles.

About the author

I was a real book worm growing up, and loved reading *The Famous Five, The Chronicles of Narnia, Watership Down* and lots more. One of the few times I didn't have my nose in a book was when my sister and I were walking our dog. He looked a lot like a wolf – which is maybe why I later wrote a book called *Wolfie* about a girl whose pet dog turns out to be a wolf! I loved reading stories so much it was no surprise I ended up writing my own.

I've really enjoyed setting Dirk in the Stone Age – and, of course, I've given him his own wolf. Like Dirk, I'm not very practical, so I'd have just the same problems as him if I were a Stone Age kid. Only I don't think I would do so well if I ever met a Snaggle-Toothed Swamp Cat!